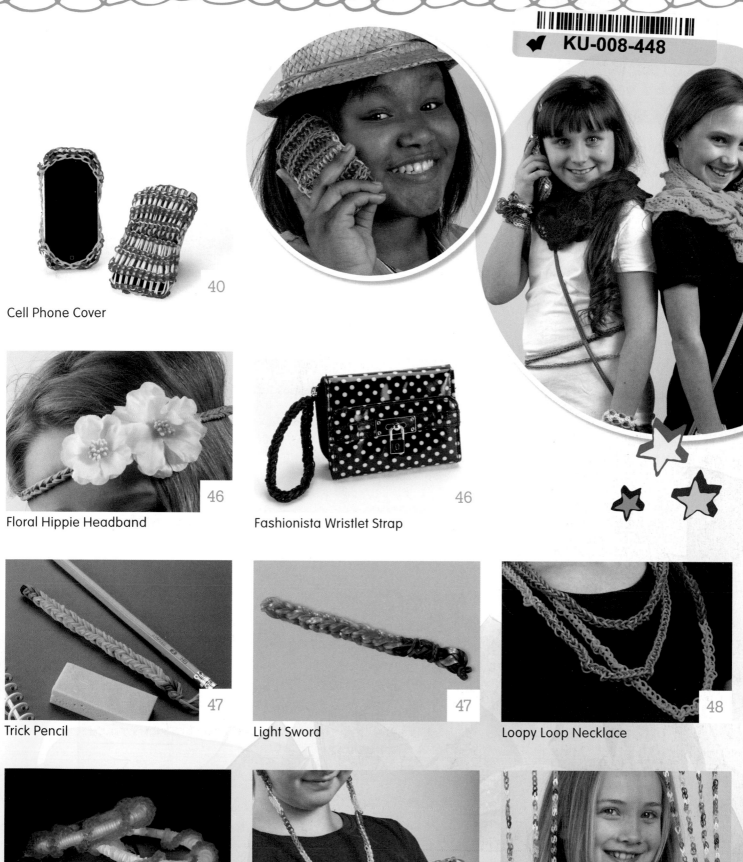

Cell Phone Cover
40

Floral Hippie Headband
46

Fashionista Wristlet Strap
46

Trick Pencil
47

Light Sword
47

Loopy Loop Necklace
48

Wrapped Glow-in-the-Dark Bracelet
48

Crazy Cool Cord Wrap
48

Glam Beaded Curtain
48

Learn the Basics

Tools and Materials

To get started, you'll need just four simple items, most of which are available at your local craft or toy store. You'll need:

> A loom for rubber band jewelry (such as Rainbow Loom®, Cra-Z-Loom™, or FunLoom™)
> Small plastic clips (C or S clips are best)
> Rubber bands (½" to ¾" in diameter)
> A small crochet hook

Looms can be purchased as kits that include all four items listed above. That's an easy way to start! When you run out of rubber bands (which is sure to happen fast!) or if you want more colors, you can scoot over to your local craft store and buy more in a rainbow of colors. Any craft store that carries the looms will carry the rubber bands and plastic clips—and you'll run out of those, too!

Different looms have different numbers of rows or columns. All the projects and diagrams in this book show the Rainbow Loom®, but don't worry if you have a different loom. Almost all of the projects in this book are compatible with looms other than the Rainbow Loom®. As long as you follow the diagrams and instructions exactly, your piece will turn out great; you may just have unused rows or columns of pegs that you can ignore.

Here's a hint: If you have a loom but no hook, it's a good idea to take the loom with you when you buy or borrow a crochet hook. You'll want to pick the size that fits perfectly into your loom! (Size G, 4.25mm, will work well.) See if your grandma or one of your mom's family friends is into crochet, and borrow one of their hooks!

There are so many colors you can use to make rubber band projects!

Beyond the basic solid colors, there are shiny bands, glittery bands, clear bands, multicolor bands, and more! Keep an eye out for the latest and coolest colors at your local craft store and online.

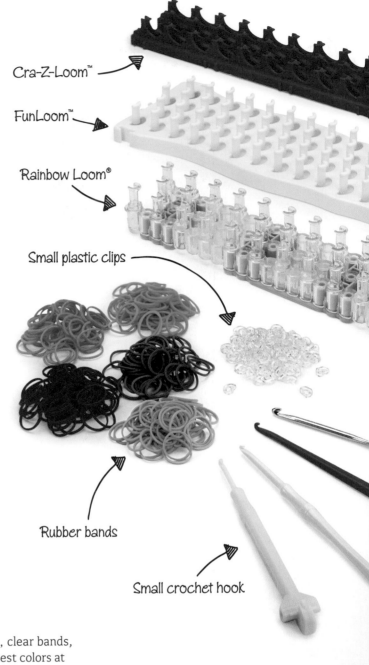

Cra-Z-Loom™

FunLoom™

Rainbow Loom®

Small plastic clips

Rubber bands

Small crochet hook

Making the Basic Bracelet on a Loom

This most basic bracelet introduces you to the loom and the general idea of placing bands and looping them. Once you get the hang of it, you'll be on your way to making tons of awesome projects! Check out the helpful diagram on page 8 as you follow these step-by-step instructions.

What You'll Need

> 25 rubber bands (for this example, 13 purple and 12 pink)
> 1 clip
> Loom
> Hook

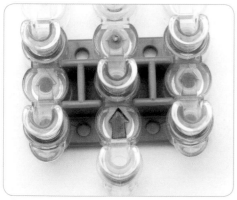

1 Turn your loom so that the arrow faces **up** (away from you); the bottom middle peg sticks out at the bottom.

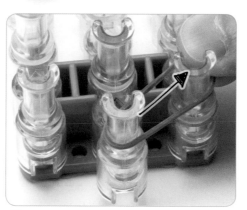

2 Place your first rubber band on the bottom middle peg (the one closest to you) and stretch it onto the bottom right peg.

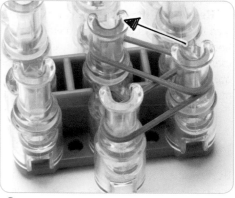

3 Place your second rubber band on the peg you just ended on and stretch it onto the peg to the upper left (the middle peg second from the bottom).

4 Place your third rubber band on the peg you just ended on and stretch it onto the peg to the upper right of it.

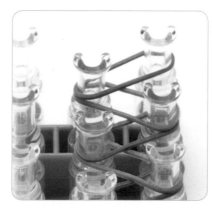

5 Keep on repeating this back-and-forth pattern until you've run out of bands or reached the top of the loom. **Always remember to start on the last peg you ended on.** Now look at the diagram and photo on page 8 and make sure that your loom looks like the pictures.

5

6 Now you are ready to loop! First, turn your loom so that the arrow at the top is facing **down** (towards you).

7 Starting at the bottom of the loom (closest to you), **push your hook down into the big loop** created by the last band you placed. Hook the second-to-last band you placed, being sure to hook it **inside the groove** on the peg.

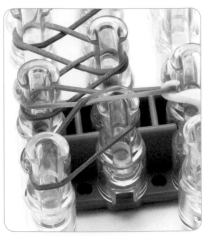

8 Lift the band off the bottom middle peg…

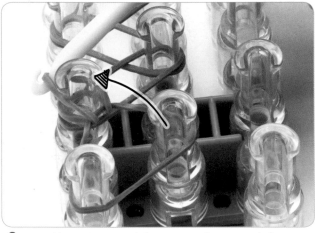

9 …and loop it around the peg to the upper left, which is the other peg that the band is also looped on. This is looping a band back to the peg it came from.

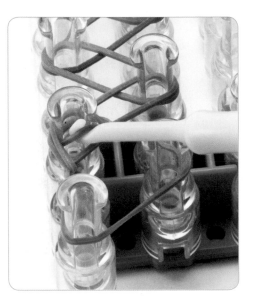

10 Now, push your hook down into the groove in the peg you just looped onto, and hook the next rubber band. Don't hook the one you just looped!

NEVER DO THIS!
Never hook a band by going around the outside as shown in this photo. **ALWAYS** push your hook down into the groove of the peg you are on, down inside the bands that are already looped there, as shown in step 10.

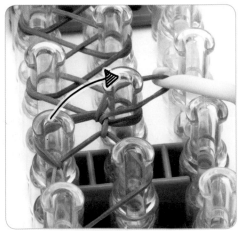

11 Lift the band off the peg and loop it back to the peg it came from.

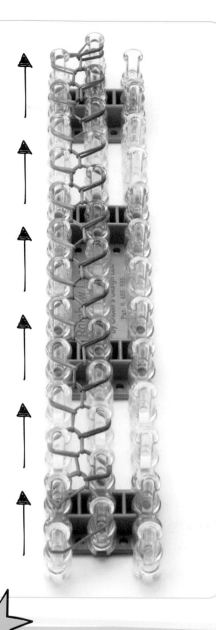

12 Keep on repeating this pattern all the way up to the top of the loom. **Always remember to push your hook down into the groove before hooking the next band.** Here's what your loom should look like after you finish all the looping! Stick with it; soon it'll become like second nature!

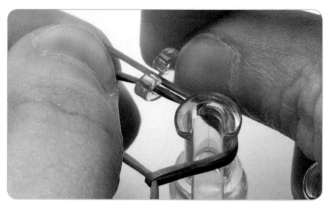

13 Take your clip and hook it around **both strands** of the one rubber band that is looped on the top middle peg, the very last band that you looped. It helps to pull the strands taut with one finger.

14 Holding the clip firmly between your fingers, pull the bracelet off the loom, one peg at a time. Don't be afraid to pull hard; it won't break!

15 Clip the rubber band on the other end onto the clip. You've made your first bracelet!

CRAFTY TIP!

Colors Galore

You can get creative with color on the very first bracelet you make! The order of your bracelet colors will match the order you place the rubber bands on the loom. If you alternate colors, you'll have an alternating bracelet; if you do three of one color at a time, you'll have stripes along your bracelet! Try laying out your 25 rubber bands in the pattern you want to see.

Understanding Diagrams

Now that you've made a basic bracelet, let's look at the diagram for the basic bracelet so that you will be able to use the diagrams in this book. For most projects, there is a **Load It Up!** diagram that you must follow in order to get your bracelet or other project started. This is called loading it or placing it on the loom. Then, you simply follow the step-by-step **Get Loopin'** instructions to make your bracelet. It's that easy!

The **Load It Up!** diagram shows you the order in which you must place your rubber bands and how your loom will look once you have finished placing all your bands. Each diagram shows a specific color arrangement; you can always change the colors, but never change the order!

Load It Up!

Take a look at this **Load It Up!** diagram for the basic bracelet. If you followed the step-by-step directions on page 5, then you followed this pattern the whole way through! Your loom should look just like the photo of the loaded loom to the right. Try making another basic bracelet by following the diagram and see if you succeed!

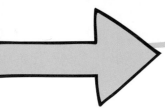

13-Purple, 12-Pink

Start at this end

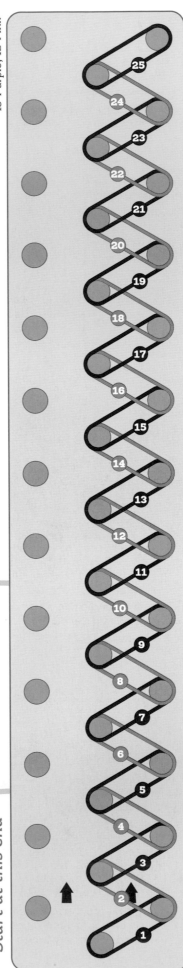

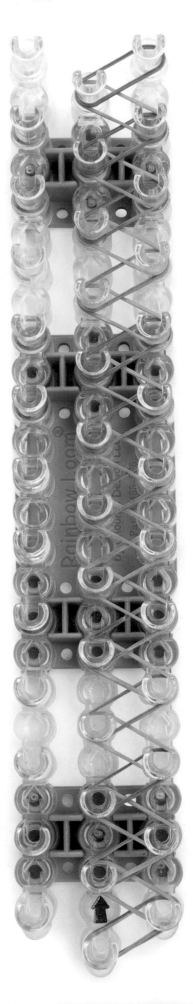

Terrific Tips and Tricks

Making Slip Knots

Many advanced projects in this book require slip knots to tie bands together. You can't shove six or eight bands into one clip very easily, and slip knots are a nice and secure way to complete a project. Here's how to make this simple but strong knot. In the example shown, you are completing a bracelet that has a whopping six strands on the last peg that need to be connected.

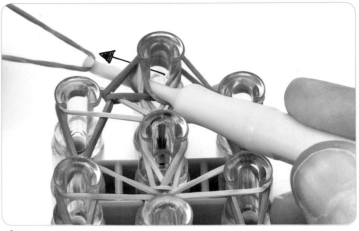

1 Dig your hook down into the groove of the last peg (or, depending on the project, through all the bands you want to connect). Grab a new band (a finishing band) and hook it onto the hook at the base of the peg where the hook comes out, as shown. Slide the other end of the band securely around your finger.

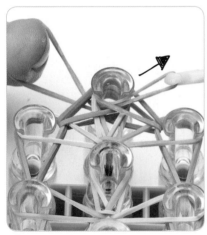

2 Pull the hook end of the band all the way up through the peg, being careful not to snag the other rubber band strands.

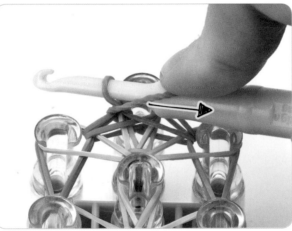

3 Loop the band on your finger onto the hook, placing it **behind** the band that's already there. Hold it down against the hook with one finger so that it doesn't get mixed up with the other loop.

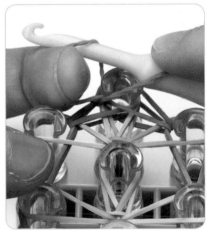

4 Grab the front loop—the one that is closest to the hook end of the hook—and slide it onto one finger…

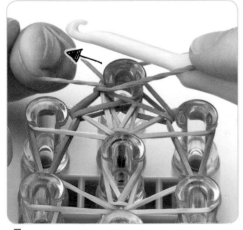

5 …then pull it off the hook, keeping it on your finger.

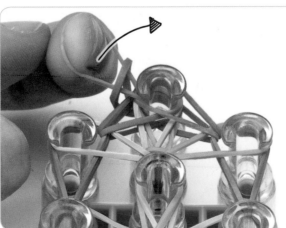

6 Now slide the remaining loop off the hook, and start to pull the loop on your finger to tighten the knot. As you pull, slide the knot around to the very top of the peg to center the knot.

Making Basic Single Links on the Hook

Many projects in this book require you to make links without the loom. These "basic links" are made on the hook, and they are very easy to learn. Just follow the steps here.

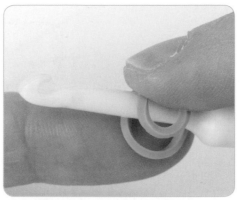

1 To start a basic link, first fold one band over your hook as shown.

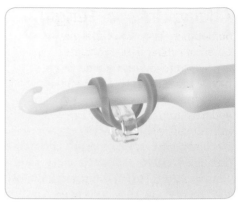

2 Clip the two loops to secure the band around your hook.

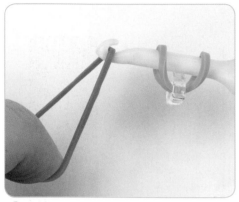

3 Hook one end of your second band on the tip of the hook, holding the other end with one finger so it is slightly taut.

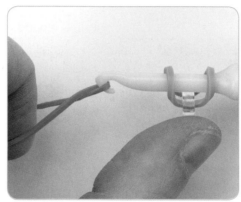

4 Rotate your hook so it faces down, making sure the clipped band doesn't rotate. Your hook and bands should look like this. Twisting your hook lets it slide through the clipped band without getting caught on the two loops.

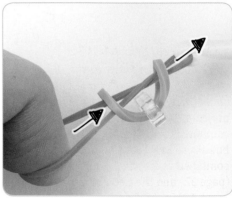

5 Carefully pull the hook, with one end of the second rubber band, all the way back through the double loop, holding onto the other end of the second band with your fingers. Don't pull the end you're holding through the double loop.

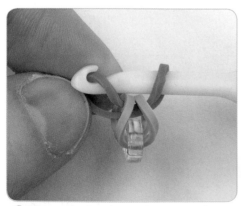

6 Rotate the hook so it faces up. Then loop the end of the band you are still holding up onto the hook. Make sure the band isn't twisted. The first clipped band will end up underneath the hook.

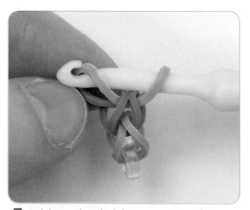

7 Add another link by repeating this process (steps 3–6) of hooking a new band, twisting your hook down, pulling the band through, twisting your hook up, and looping the other end of the band onto the hook.

8 Now continue making as many links as you need to! You can even make an entire bracelet this way by making 25 basic links in a row.

Adding Links for Length

Sometimes, because of the way different rubber band bracelets are looped together, they don't have as much stretch and won't fit your wrist. If you come up short, you have two options: you can either make the bracelet longer by combining two looms (see Combining Looms below), or you can simply add basic links to extend the bracelet. Because most of us don't have two looms, adding basic links is the solution—and it's super easy! Here's how.

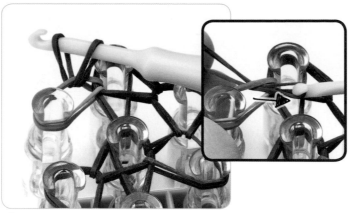

1 Pull one end of a new band through the final band or set of bands where you want to extend the bracelet, just as you would when making a basic link (see page 10). Loop the end of the band you are holding up onto the hook.

2 Keep adding links this way until your bracelet is as long as you want it to be.

Combining Looms

You can combine many looms end-to-end (lengthwise) or side-to-side (widthwise) to make longer or wider projects. Most looms are easy to combine lengthwise (far right), but not all looms can be correctly combined widthwise. For the Robot (page 32) and the Cell Phone Cover (page 40) in this book, you will need to combine your looms with the pegs in an alternating pattern (left); a Rainbow Loom® can be arranged this way. Note: You can't just place two looms next to one another and not change the peg columns around (middle)—that won't work.

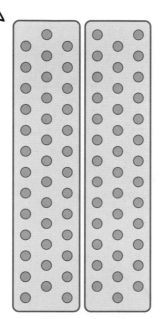
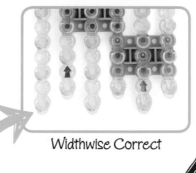

Widthwise Correct

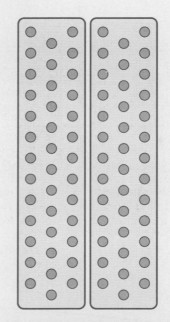
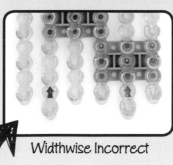

Widthwise Incorrect

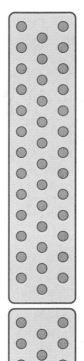

Lengthwise Correct

Vine Bracelet

This bracelet is super customizable! You can add beads, double or triple the bands, and even twist the bands in various ways to create many different bracelets with just one design. Have fun with it!

Blossoming Vine
(1 band per ring)

Blossoming Vine
(3 bands per ring)

Baseball Beads

Figure Eights

What You'll Need

○ **34**
Pink bands (vine)

○ **10, 20, or 30**
Lime green bands (rings)

⊙ **1**
Clip

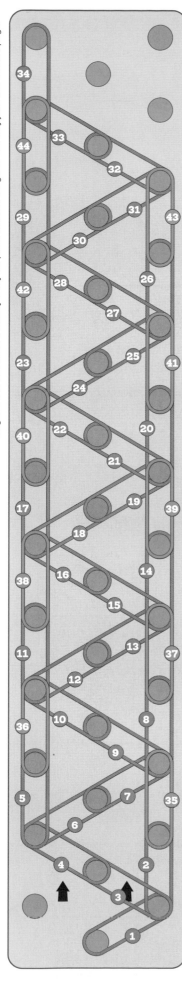

Load It Up!

First, place the 34 "vine" bands as shown in the diagram. It's like a zigzag, but with an extra up-and-down band at each corner. Make sure you place the extra up-and-down band first before continuing to zig and zag to the left and right. Once you've placed all 34 vine bands, add the "ring" bands where shown to fill in the holes, starting with band 35 near the bottom of the loom. You can use one, two, three, or more bands at once for the ring bands—it's up to you! (The diagram shows a single ring band design.)

Get Loopin'

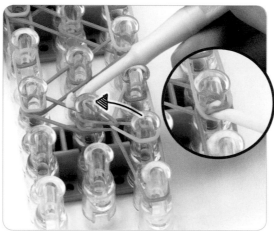

1 Turn the loom so the arrow faces down. Hook the bottom band on the second from bottom right peg and loop it up to the second from bottom middle peg. Be sure to push your hook down into the peg, inside the last ring band you placed, to hook the band.

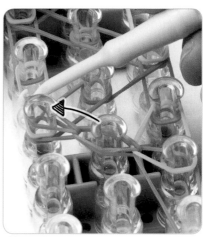

2 Push your hook down into the peg and hook the bottom band on the second from bottom middle peg, where you just ended. Loop it to the peg to the upper left of it.

3 Then, starting from the peg you just ended on, loop the next two bottom bands diagonally up and to the right, like you did in steps 1–2.

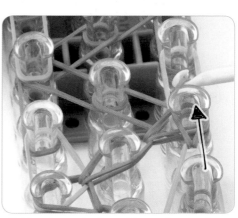

4 Now loop the band from the third from bottom right peg up to the fourth from bottom right peg. This is the band that shares a peg with the top of the ring band closest to you. The ring bands do not get looped.

13

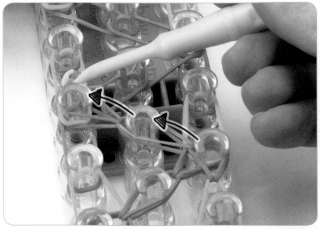

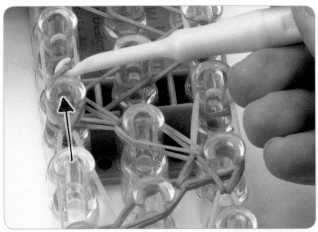

5 Now, starting from the peg you just ended on, loop the next two bottom bands, diagonally up and to the left, like you did in step 3. The first band goes from the right column to the center column; the second band goes from the center column to the left column.

6 As in step 4, loop the band that shares a peg with the top of the second ring band up to the peg above it. This is looping the band from the fourth from bottom left peg to the fifth from bottom left peg.

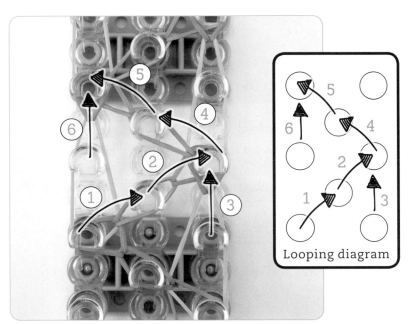

Looping diagram

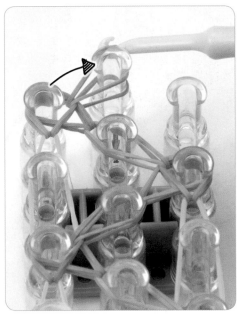

7 Repeat the pattern in steps 3–6 for the rest of the bracelet, following the zigzag path you made when you placed the bands. Always loop two bands diagonally up and across ① ②, then loop up the band that connects the next ring band ③. Use the looping diagram as a guide.

8 Loop the bottom band from the top left peg to the top middle peg, add a clip, and pull your bracelet off the loom.

CRAFTY TIP!

Don't get frustrated if your bracelet (or other project) doesn't work out the first time you try to make it. Just try again and see where you went wrong. You'll get the hang of it!

44-Black, 10-Beads

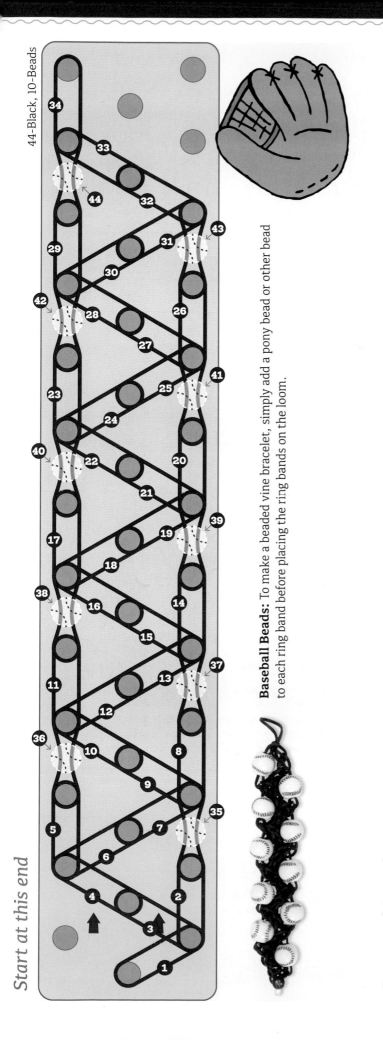

Baseball Beads: To make a beaded vine bracelet, simply add a pony bead or other bead to each ring band before placing the ring bands on the loom.

34-Turquoise, 10-Purple

Figure Eights: Figure eights are a lot of fun! When placing the ring bands on the loom, twist them once to make a figure eight between the two pegs the ring bands are stretched on. That's all there is to it!

15

Penguin

An adorable penguin can be used as a charm, toy, backpack fob, or just for decoration. With surprisingly simple techniques, you can make a whole flock of flightless birds in a range of real-life species!

What You'll Need

84
Gray bands
(58 body, 26 wings)

12
White bands (body)

6
Orange bands (feet)

1
Pony bead (beak)

2
Gray finishing bands

Load It Up!

Place the bands for the penguin body on the loom according to the diagram. Be sure to follow the order exactly, and don't miss any bands. Be sure to note which bands are double bands (two bands placed at the same time on the same pegs) and which bands are single. Don't forget to add a double-looped band at the top middle peg of the loom (band 76). There's nothing tricky about this: just loop the band onto the peg, then twist it and loop it on again, as if you are tying a ponytail with a hair elastic.

Before You Begin

To make the penguin, first you need to make its wings separately and attach them later. The wings are made up of 13 bands total for each wing. Start the penguin by making the wings as shown below. Then load your bands on the loom as shown in the diagram, placing the two wings on the pegs marked in the diagram.

Get Loopin': Make the Wings

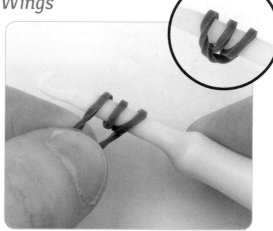

1 Start by triple looping one band onto your hook. That means put it around the hook, then twist it and loop it on again, then twist it and loop it on one more time. That makes three loops around the hook, or a triple loop.

76 Wrapped 2x

Attach Wing

Attach Wing

Start at this end

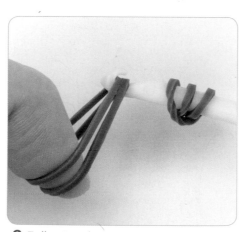

2 Following the instructions on page 10, create six links on the hook, but use **two bands** for each link. These are called double band links. So, you need 12 bands to make six double band links. Make sure that for the first link you pull the two bands through all three loops on the hook.

3 Once you have finished each wing (make two), there's no need for a clip—just stick the wings on the very top pegs of the loom until you are ready to place them. If you haven't already, load the penguin body on the loom; then place the wings where shown on the diagram.

Get Loopin': Make the Penguin

4 Make sure you have added the wings to the loom before starting. Turn the loom so the arrow faces down. First, push your hook down into the bottom middle peg, inside the double-looped band, hook the top three orange bands (the left foot), and loop them up to the left. Then push your hook down inside the double-looped band, hook the three remaining orange bands (the right foot), and loop them up to the right.

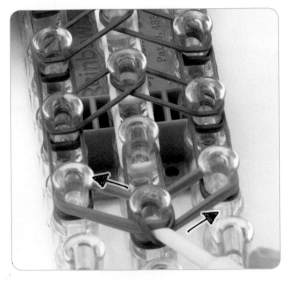

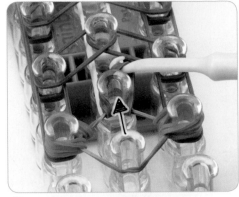

5 Hook and loop the bottom two gray bands from the bottom middle peg up to the peg above them. Make sure you hook them from inside the double-looped band.

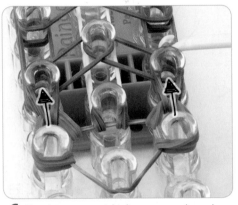

6 On the pegs with the orange bands looped onto them, hook and loop each set of bottom two gray bands up to the pegs above them. Make sure you push your hook down into the groove and hook them from inside all the orange bands.

7 Now, moving back to the center column, hook and loop the next pair of center (white) bands to the peg above them.

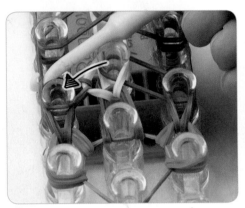

8 Hook the top single gray "spine" band from the peg you just looped to, and loop it to the peg down and to the left of it. Make sure you hook the correct spine band (the top one).

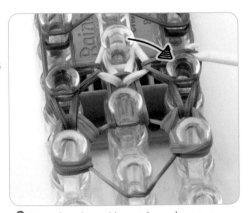

9 Now hook and loop the other gray spine band the same way, down and to the right. Be careful not to let the band fall off the hook.

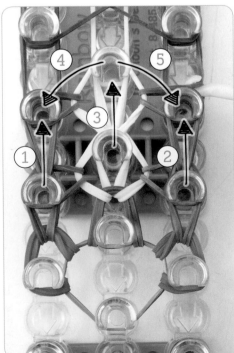

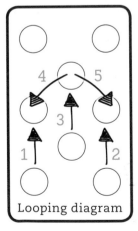

Looping diagram

10 Repeat this pattern for the rest of the penguin's belly: loop each pair of bottom side bands up to pegs above them ① ②, then loop the center pair of bands up to the peg above them ③; then loop each single spine band down and to the left ④ and right ⑤, one at a time. Use the diagram as a guide.

11 Once you have looped the last of the single spine bands, hook and loop the last two bottom sets of side bands (the gray bands that go up and down) up onto the pegs with the wings on them. Then hook and loop the last set of center bands (gray) up onto the peg above them.

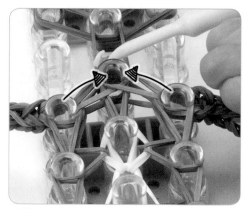

12 Now loop each of the bottom sets of gray bands from the pegs with the wings on them up and in towards the center. Be sure to push your hook down into the peg, inside all the wing bands.

13 Hook and loop the bottom set of gray bands on the center peg up to the peg above them, the bottom peg of the head. You'll really have to dig in with your hook to hook the neck bands because there will now be a ton of bands on the peg you're starting from.

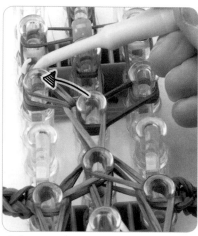

14 Hook the top set of unlooped gray bands (top not counting the neck bands you just looped up onto this peg) on the center bottom peg of the head and loop them up and to the left.

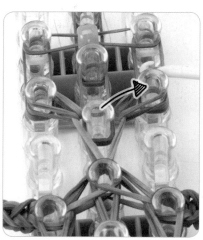

15 Hook the new top set of unlooped gray bands on the center bottom peg of the head and loop them up and to the right.

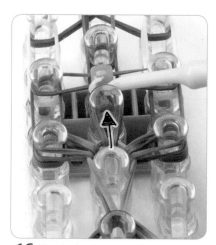

16 Hook the last set of gray bands on the center bottom peg of the head and loop them up to the peg above them.

17 Hook and loop the first two bottom sets of gray side bands and the next bottom set of center gray bands of the head, and loop them all to the pegs above them.

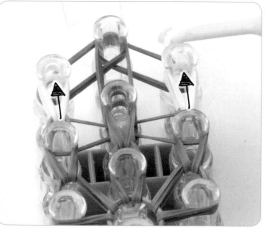

18 Hook and loop the next two sets of white side bands, the eyes, up to the pegs above them. Make sure you push your hook down inside the beaded band. The beaded band doesn't get looped.

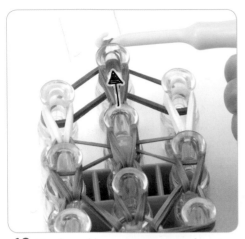  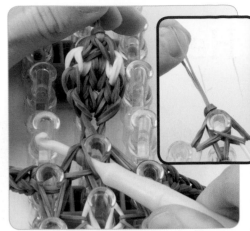

19 Hook and loop the last set of center gray bands on the head up to the peg above them, the top middle peg.

20 Hook and loop the last two bottom sets of gray bands from the top left and right pegs up to the top middle peg.

21 Make a double slip knot (a slip knot with two bands at once) around all the bands on the top middle peg. Carefully remove the penguin from the loom, using your hook to help.

Crested Penguin

To make a crested penguin with yellow feathers on its head, you need four yellow bands. Simply push your hook through the gray or black bands above the eyes (bands 1–4 from the diagram) from the front to the back, pull two yellow bands through at once, make a slip knot with both bands at once, and then snip the loops of the slip knots at the very top. You've made funky crest feathers!

Emperor Penguin

To make the black emperor penguin, make the bands right underneath the eyes a mix of orange and yellow (one of each) instead of black, and make most of the belly white instead of making just a stripe of white. (The under-eye bands are bands 13–16 from the diagram.)

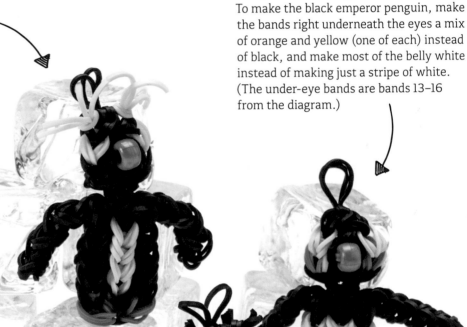

Baby Penguin

The baby penguin is just a miniature version of the regular penguin. Follow the photo for an idea of how large (how many rows) to make it. If you want to add extra fuzzy feathers at the top as shown, add four double-band slip knots at the top of its head, two on each side above the eyes, and snip them very short (see the instructions for the crested penguin for more on this).

Headphones Slider Bead

Use the fishtail technique with six pegs to make a fully functional slider bead for your headphones. You'll be able to easily shorten and lengthen your headphone cords to fit comfortably and add flair to an otherwise boring accessory!

What You'll Need

12
Turquoise bands

12
Yellow bands

12
Neon orange bands

1 Pair
Headphones (with small or flexible earbuds)

You can also use an EZ Looper™ by Pepperell Braiding Company to make this project!

21

Before You Begin

Every pair of headphones is different, and some headphones are more delicate than others when it comes to pulling on the cords to slide the bead up and down. The slider bead is pretty tight, so here are some tips! **Don't use sticky bands** to make the bead—stick with normal colors instead of shiny, jelly, or gummy-textured bands. **If you're worried about breaking your headphones,** pull the cord all the way through the bead, past where it splits for the earbuds, at step 3 (below). It will take longer to make the bead because you'll have to thread each band around a longer length of cord instead of just the plug, but you'll be sure to keep your cord safe. Also consider starting from the split in the cord if the plastic slider bead that is built into your headphones is large—it will be difficult to pull the rubber band slider bead over it if this is the case.

Get Loopin'

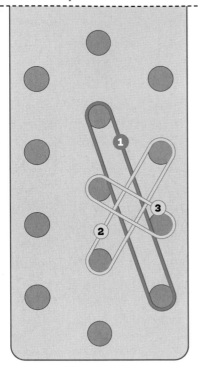

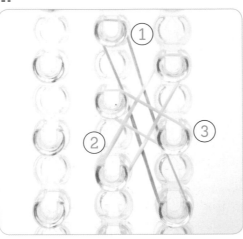

1 Place the first layer of three bands on six pegs as shown. Lay one band at a time, going clockwise from the most stretched band (on the two pegs farthest apart) to the least stretched band (on the two pegs next to each other horizontally).

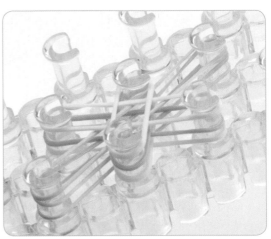

2 Place two additional layers exactly as you did the first layer so there are three bands on each pair of pegs. (For color pattern ideas, see page 25.) Make sure you don't overlap any bands—you'll need to know which band is on the bottom.

3 Push the plug end of the headphones up through the hole created in the very middle of all the layered bands so that the entire plug (an inch or so) sticks out of the top layer. Push the headphones in through the side, not through the bottom.

4 Hook the bottom band on the top left peg...

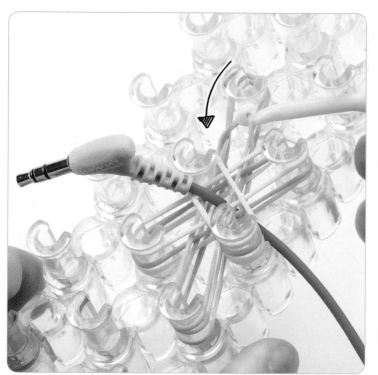

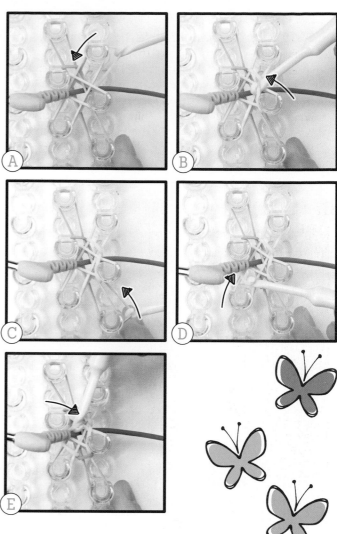

5 …and unloop it up and over the peg from the outside to the inside. Going clockwise, hook and unloop the bottom band on each of the six pegs this way, one at a time. When you are done, there will only be two bands left looped around each peg.

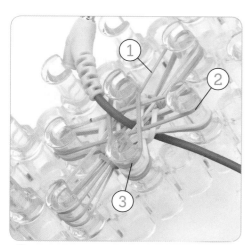

6 Push down all the bands on all the pegs, and then place another single layer of three bands as you did in step 1. **Make sure each band goes around the headphones plug.**

7 Hook and unloop the new bottom layer on all six pegs as you did in steps 4–5. Make sure you haven't overlapped any bands and are unlooping the correct band on each peg.

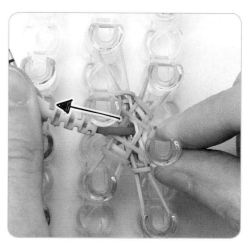

8 Push down all the bands on all the pegs, and then pull the plug end of the headphones up slightly to make sure it isn't stuck in the bands. You can always pull it up later, but it will be more difficult if you let it get too covered by looped bands.

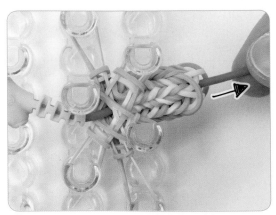

9 Add and unloop eight more layers one layer at a time, always being sure to loop each band around the headphones when you add the layer. As it starts to get crowded underneath the pegs, tug on the cord to pull the slider bead out towards the side of the loom.

10 When you are done, you will have added 12 layers total to the loom, but only unlooped ten total. You will have two unlooped layers left on the loom (layers 11 and 12).

11 To start finishing the slider bead, hook and unloop the bottom layer of bands (layer 11) without adding another layer of bands on top. You'll end up with only one band looped on each peg (layer 12).

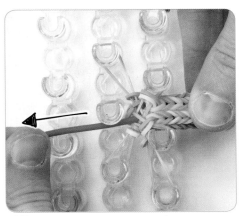

12 Holding the bead down with your fingers, pull the headphones cord up through the bead, past where the cord splits into two. It is important to **do this now** while the bead is still on the loom.

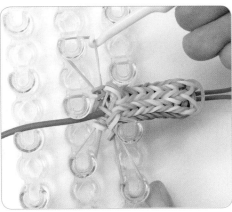

13 Now it's time to finish the bead. Start by hooking the band on the top left peg.

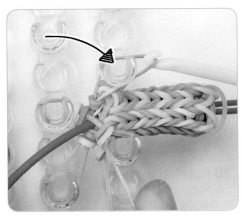

14 Carefully transfer the band you hooked onto the next peg clockwise that has a band on it; in this case, it's the top right peg. You'll probably want to use the hook and your fingers to make the transfer.

15 Hook the bottom band on the peg you just transferred to, and unloop it up and over the peg from the outside to the inside.

16 Now transfer the same transferred band (the remaining band on the top right peg) onto the next peg clockwise (the middle right peg), just as you did in step 14.

17 Hook and unloop the bottom band on the middle right peg as you did in step 15.

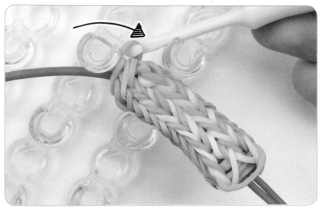

18 Repeat this process of transferring and unlooping until you only have one band left on the middle left peg.

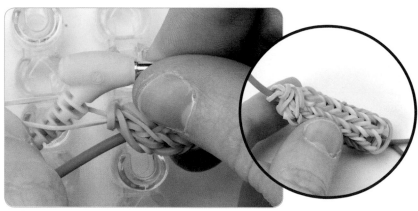

19 Loop the only band left up and over the headphones plug and slide it all the way down against the bead to complete the bottom of the bead. Take your bead off the loom.

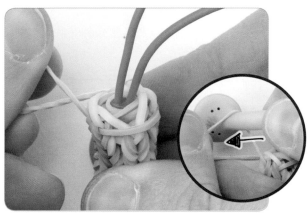

20 Now we'll tighten up the top loops. Pinch one of the two loose loops of the outermost (loosest) band at the top end of the bead and twist it into a figure eight. Feed one earbud **outward** through the top hole of the figure eight.

21 Pull the cord all the way through. You will have a neat loop at the top end of the bead around one of the two earbud cords.

22 Repeat this twist-and-pull with the other earbud for the other half of the loose loop at the top of the bead.

Color Ideas

Ⓐ **Long Stripes:** Make vertical stripes by making every layer the same, but with a different color for each of the three bands in each layer.

Ⓑ **Mixed Up:** Make a mixed and stripe design (shown in the step-by-step instructions) by always using the same color for the first band in every layer, and, for the other two bands, using two of the same color, alternating colors every layer.

Ⓒ **Color Blocks:** To make horizontal stripes, use one color per layer for four layers, then switch to a different color.

Ⓐ Ⓑ Ⓒ

Double the Fun Hand Accessory

This hand accessory combines the ideas from the Rockin' Ring and Bracelet and the Triple the Fun Bracelet (from *Totally Awesome Rubber Band Jewelry*) into a cool new design! (And you don't need the first book to learn how to make it!) After mastering this piece, try adapting other bracelets into hand accessories.

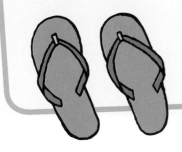

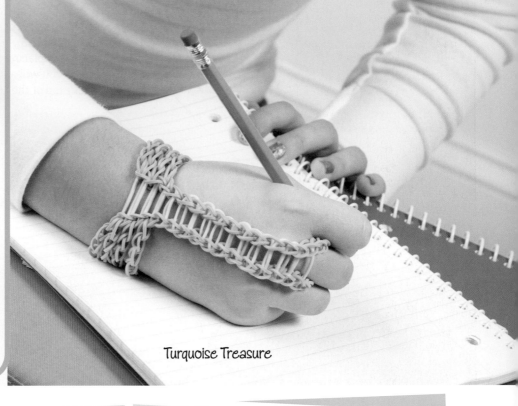

Turquoise Treasure

What You'll Need

◯ **114**
Turquoise bands (10 ring, 32 hand, 72 bracelets)

◯ **15**
Yellow bands (stripes)

◉ **8**
Clips

Knight's Gauntlet

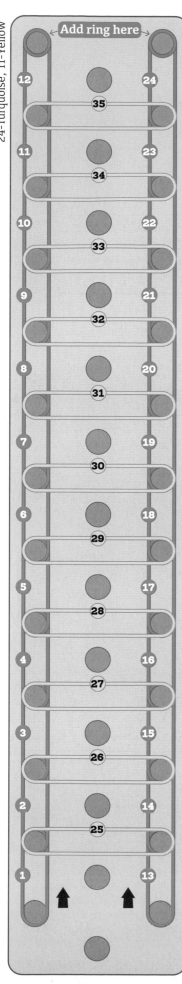

Add ring here

Start at this end

Load It Up!

Load your loom as shown, first placing the main bands of the accessory in two columns all the way up to the top (bands 1–24), then placing the stripe bands (bands 25–35). Be sure to skip the bottom and top pairs of pegs when placing the stripe bands. Once you have loaded these bands, you will add the ring that you'll make in steps 1–2 to the very top of the loom.

Get Loopin'

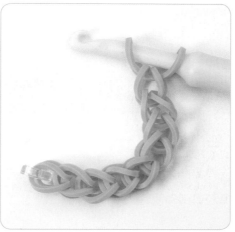

1 Make a single band chain of 10 bands on the hook using the technique shown on page 10. Be sure to fold the first band of the chain over the hook and clip it to secure it.

2 After 10 links, clip the working end of the chain to secure it, and set it aside. This is the ring part of the accessory. Now, **load your loom** according to the diagram if you haven't already.

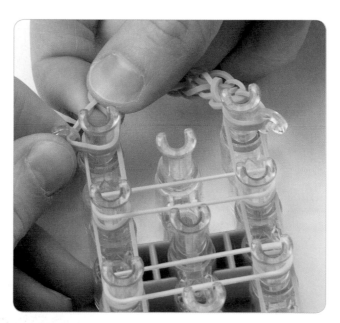

3 At the very top of the loaded loom, add one end of the ring chain you made in steps 1–2 to the top left peg and the other end of the ring chain to the top right peg. Make sure both loops of the bands on each end of the chain go onto the pegs. Remove the clips.

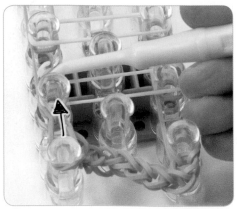

4 Turn the loom so the arrow faces down. Hook the bottom band on the bottom left peg and loop it onto the peg above it. Make sure to push your hook down into the groove, inside the ring bands on that peg.

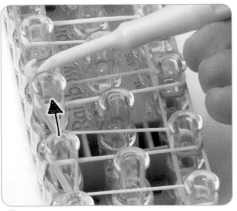

5 Continue looping all the bottom bands up the left side, all the way to the top. Make sure you always push your hook down into the groove, inside the stripe bands, to hook the bands.

6 Add a clip to the final looped band at the top left, securing both loops of the band together.

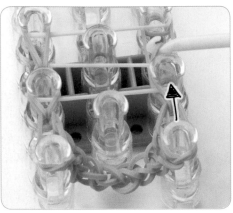

7 As in step 4, hook the bottom band on the bottom right peg and loop it onto the peg above it. Make sure to push your hook down into the groove, inside the ring bands on that peg.

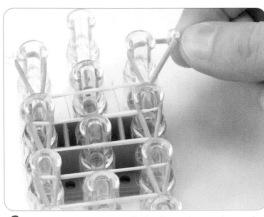

8 Continue looping all the bands up the right side, all the way to the top. Make sure you always push your hook down into the groove, inside the stripe bands, to hook the bands. Add a clip to the final looped band at the top right as you did in step 6.

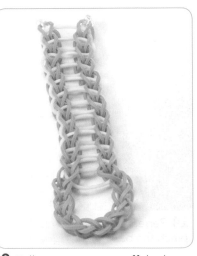

9 Pull your accessory off the loom. You'll have two clipped ends to work with now.

NOTE: If you have smaller hands, you don't need to make the accessory any longer! Just put the ring on your middle finger, hold the piece against your hand and see if it reaches comfortably to your wrist. If you think it does, jump straight to step 18! If you want to make the accessory a little longer on your hand and only have one loom, follow steps 10–17 to make the accessory four stripes longer. If you want to make the accessory a little longer and you have more than one loom, simply connect your two looms end to end to make the bracelet four stripes longer from the very beginning, and skip steps 10–17.

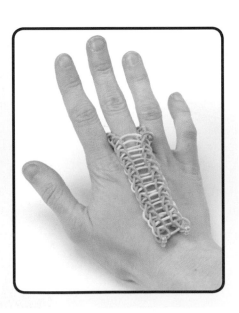

10 Load your loom as you did to make the accessory the first time, but this time with only four bands per side and three stripes, as shown. Load these bands at the top of the loom with the arrow facing up. Don't add stripes to the bottom or top pairs of pegs.

11 Pinch the base of one of the two clipped links on the piece you set aside and remove the clip. Keeping the link securely pinched, place the bottom loop of the link onto the top left peg. Make sure you have aligned the piece as shown in the photo, with the other clipped link to the right.

12 While still holding onto the other half of the link, place a stripe band around that top left peg, letting it hang loose on the peg.

13 Finally, place the other loop you are pinching onto that top left peg. This is what the peg should look like.

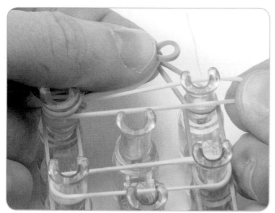

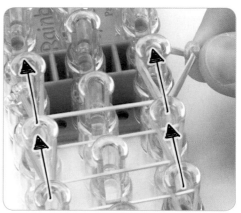

14 Repeat this process for the right side: pinch the base of the right link, remove the clip, place the bottom loop of the pinched link on the top right peg, then place the other side of the **same** stripe band that you added in step 12, and finally place the other loop of the pinched link.

15 This is what your loom should look like when you have finished both sides.

16 Turn the loom so the arrow faces down, loop up each side just as you did for the accessory originally, and clip the two bands at the top. Make sure that you are always pushing your hook down into the groove, inside all the other bands.

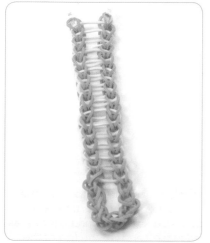

18 Now you'll make the four bracelets. Starting with the clipped bands, add nine single links to each of the four bottom **side bands** on each side (not to the stripe bands). That's a total of 72 new links.

17 Pull the accessory off the loom. You won't be able to tell where you connected the pieces!

19 Connect each half of each of the four bracelets to complete the accessory, and try it on!

Fringe Bracelet/Scrunchie

This super simple accessory can be used as a bracelet or a hair scrunchie! It's made with two columns of bands connected by horizontal bands that aren't looped, similar to the Double the Fun Hand Accessory on page 26.

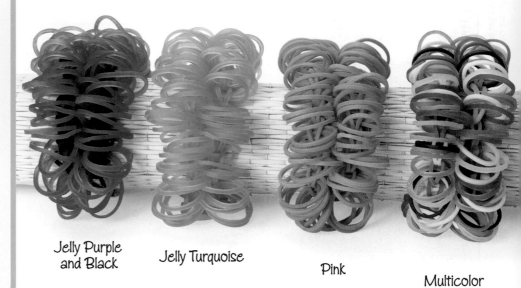

Jelly Purple and Black

Jelly Turquoise

Pink

Multicolor

What You'll Need

○ **39**
Black bands (base)

○ **104**
Jelly Purple bands (fringe)

○ **1**
Black finishing band

○ **1**
Clip

Start at this end

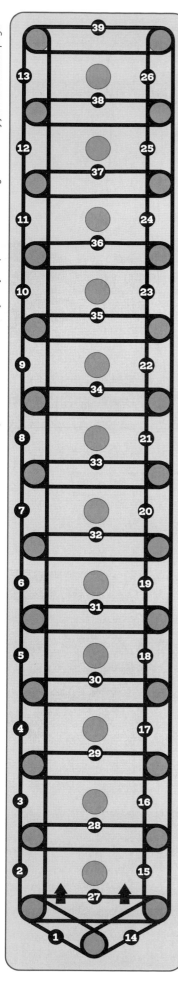

Load It Up!

Place the side columns (bands 1–26) first, then place the horizontal stripe bands starting near the bottom of the loom (bands 27–39). You'll be adding the fringe bands as you loop.

Get Loopin'

1 Turn the loom so the arrow faces down. Place four loose bands onto your hook near the tip.

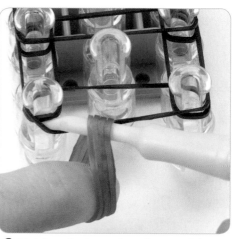

2 Holding the loose bands out of the way, push your hook down into the bottom left peg to hook the bottom band from inside the stripe band.

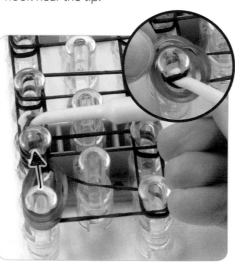

3 Slide the four loose bands down off the hook and onto the peg. Now loop the band you have hooked up to the peg above it. This pulls the link all the way through the four loose bands.

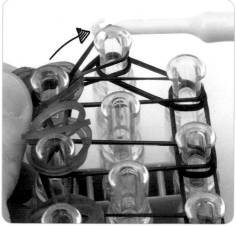

4 Repeat this process for all the links on both columns, adding four loose bands to every link, including when you loop the bands from the top left and right pegs onto the top middle peg. Slip knot the top bands together, pull the piece off the loom, clip the ends together, and you're done!

Robot

This is the coolest figure you'll ever make out of rubber bands! With nifty accents like a green heart button, an antenna, and hinged, poseable arms, you'll have so much fun with one robot that you'll definitely want to make him a pal.

What You'll Need

○ **173**
Gray bands
(24 arms, 32 legs, 117 body)

○ **32**
Black bands
(10 arms, 10 legs, 12 body)

○ **8**
Yellow bands
(5 stomach, 3 antenna)

○ **2**
Lime green bands (heart)

○ **5**
Red bands (mouth and eyes)

○ **8**
Clips

Dude!
...not cool.

Before You Begin

You have to make the arms and legs separately. Start the robot by making the arms and legs as shown below.

Wrapped 3x

Start at this end

Load It Up! Arms

First load your loom with the bands to make one arm as shown to the right. Place two bands at once where the numbers are doubled (bands 1–16). The last band you place is a single band looped **three** times around the top left peg (see the Load It Up! diagram on page 17 for more detail). You have to make two arms, so you can load the second arm on your loom now, placing it a few pegs above the first arm.

Get Loopin': Make the Arms

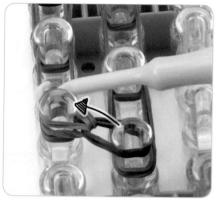

1 Turn the loom so the arrow faces down. Push your hook down into the groove of the bottom right peg, inside the triple-wrapped black band, and hook the top two gray bands that stretch up to the left. Loop the bands up and to the left.

2 Hook and loop the bottom two bands on each left peg onto the peg above them for the entire left column. Clip the loops on the top left peg. Refer to the looping diagram (right) as a guide.

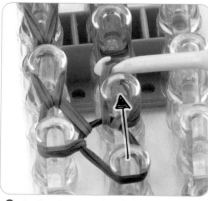

3 Go back to the bottom right peg, push your hook down into the groove of the peg, inside the triple-wrapped black band, and hook the two bottom bands that stretch up to the peg above. Loop the bands up to the peg above.

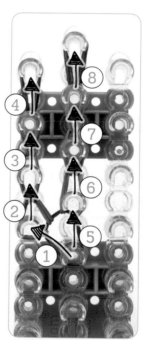

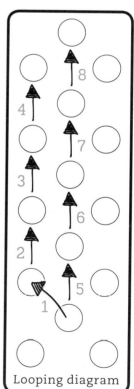

Looping diagram

4 Hook and loop the bottom two bands on each right peg onto the peg above them for the entire right column. Clip the loops on the top right peg. Refer to the looping diagram (right) as a guide. Remove your first arm from the loom, then make a second arm to match.

Load It Up! Legs

First load your loom with the bands to make one leg as shown to the right. Place two bands at once where the numbers are doubled (bands 1–16). At the top, bands 17 and 18 are single bands looped **three** times around their respective pegs (see the Load It Up! diagram on page 17 for more detail). Finally, place bands 19–21, which are single bands looped **twice** around **two** pegs. You have to make two legs, so you can load the second leg on your loom now, placing it a few pegs above the first leg.

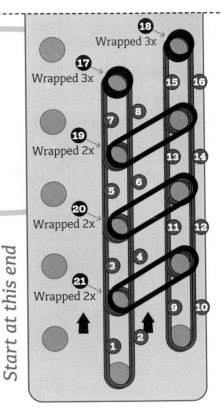

Get Loopin': Make the Legs

1 Turn the loom so the arrow faces down. Push your hook down into the groove of the bottom left peg, inside the triple-wrapped black band, and hook the two bottom bands that stretch up to the peg above. Loop the bands up to the peg above.

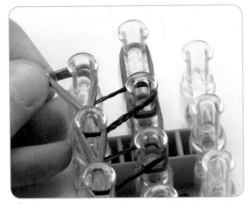

2 Hook and loop the rest of the bands on the left column, always making sure to push your hook down into the groove of the pegs (inside the horizontal black bands) to hook the bottom bands. When you have looped the entire column, clip the loops on the top left peg. Refer to the looping diagram (right) as a guide.

3 On the bottom right peg, push your hook down into the groove of the peg, inside the triple-wrapped black band, and hook the two bottom bands that stretch up to the peg above. Loop the bands up to the peg above.

4 Hook and loop the rest of the bands on the right column, always making sure to push your hook down into the groove of the pegs (inside the horizontal black bands) to hook the bottom bands. When you have looped the entire column, clip the loops on the top right peg. Refer to the looping diagram (right) as a guide. Remove your first leg from the loom, then make a second leg to match.

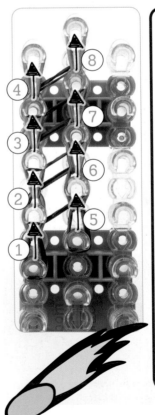

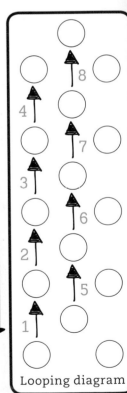

Looping diagram

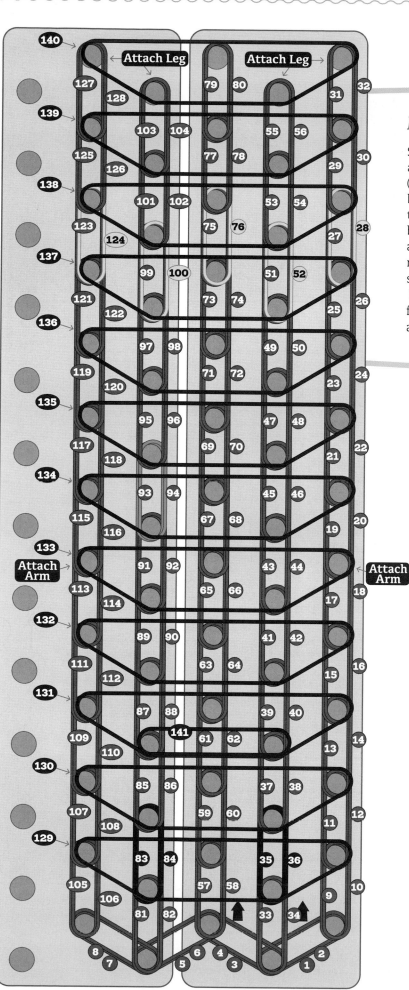

Bands:

120-Gray, 12-Black, 2-Lime Green, 5-Yellow, 5-Red

Start at this end

Load It Up! Body

Start by placing double bands along the bottom of the loom (bands 1–8). Next, starting at the bottom right, place double bands in exactly the color pattern shown to make most of the robot's body (bands 9–128). (For the yellow stomach, place a gray and a yellow band together.) Then, starting near the bottom of the loom, place 12 single bands stretched around sets of five pegs (bands 129–140). Finally, add a red band to the middle of the robot's face where shown (band 141). Now add the arms and legs to the pegs indicated.

Bands 1–8

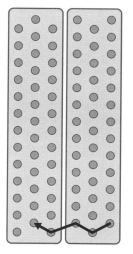

Bands 9–128

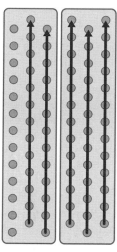

Bands 129–140

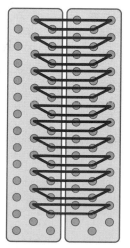

Band 141

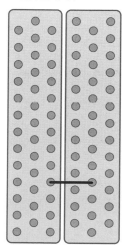

35

Get Loopin': Make the Robot

1 **Make sure you have added the arms and legs to the loom before starting.** Turn the loom so the arrow faces down. Push your hook down into the groove of the bottom right peg, inside all the leg bands and the horizontal black band, and hook the two bottom bands.

2 Loop the bands up to the peg directly above them.

3 Hook and loop the entire right column this way, all the way to the top. Always remember to push your hook down into the grooves of the pegs, inside the horizontal black bands, to hook the bottom bands. Take extra care to hook from inside all the arm bands on the peg where you attached the right arm!

4 Push your hook down into the groove of the bottom second from right peg, inside all the leg bands, and hook the two bottom bands. Loop the bands up to the peg directly above them.

5 Hook and loop the second from right column this way only up to where you placed the mouth band—**stop before hooking and looping the band that would cover up the mouth band.**

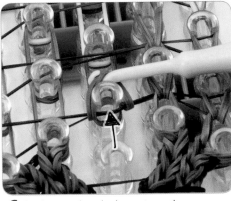

6 Push your hook down into the groove of the bottom middle peg, inside the horizontal black band, and hook the two bottom bands. Loop the bands up to the peg directly above them. **Careful, they are loose and might fall off.**

7 Hook and loop the middle column this way only up to where you placed the mouth band. **Stop before hooking and looping the band that would cover up the mouth band.** Remember to push your hook down into the grooves of the pegs, inside the horizontal black bands.

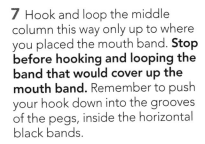

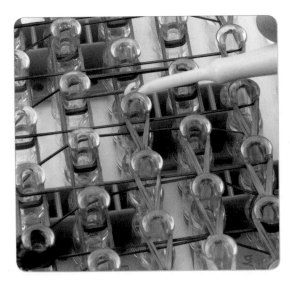

8 Push your hook down into the groove of the bottom second from left peg, inside all the leg bands, and hook the two bottom bands. Loop the bands up to the peg directly above them.

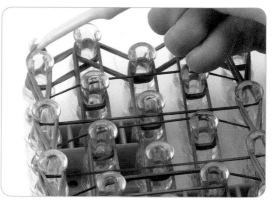

9 Hook and loop the second from left column this way only up to where you placed the mouth band. **Stop before hooking and looping the band that would cover up the mouth band.**

10 Push your hook down into the groove of the bottom left peg, inside all the leg bands and the horizontal black band, and hook the two bottom bands. Loop them up to the peg directly above them.

11 Hook and loop the entire left column this way, all the way to the top. Always remember to push your hook down into the grooves of the pegs, inside the horizontal black bands, to hook the bottom bands. Take extra care to hook from inside all the arm bands on the peg where you attached the left arm!

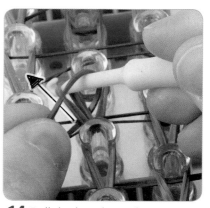

12 Now go to where you stopped before the red mouth band on the second from left column. Remove the mouth band from the loom and hold it between your fingers with the loop sticking out.

13 Hook the bands where you stopped on the second from left column. Hold the red mouth band right above that peg.

14 Pull the bands you have hooked off the peg and push them through the red mouth band.

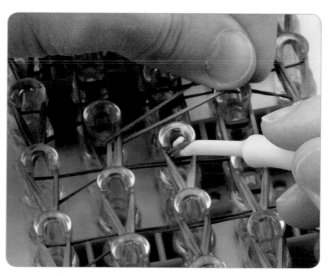

16 Repeat this process on the middle column where you stopped before. So, first, stretch the red mouth band right above the peg where you stopped on the middle column, and hook the last unlooped bands on that peg.

15 Loop the bands through the red mouth band and onto the peg directly above them. This pins the mouth band against the loom, between the bands.

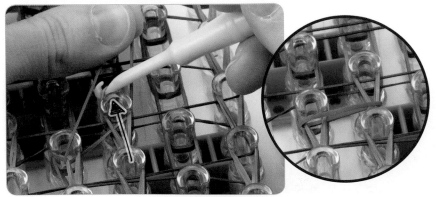

17 Pull the bands you have hooked off the peg and push them through the red mouth band. Loop the bands onto the peg directly above them.

18 Repeat this process once more on the second from right column where you stopped before to complete the mouth. You'll have to stretch the mouth band far over to the right. The last set of bands is the trickiest to loop.

19 As you did on all the columns before stopping at the mouth, hook and loop all the remaining up-and-down sets of bands on the three middle columns, all the way to the top of loom. There are eight more sets of bands left to hook and loop upwards. Always remember to push your hook down into the grooves of the pegs, inside the horizontal black bands, to hook the bottom bands.

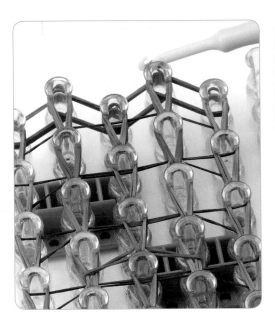

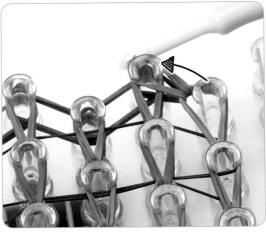

20 Now it's time to loop along the top. Hook the two bands on the top right peg and loop them up to the left.

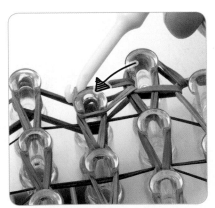

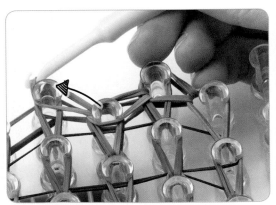

21 Push your hook down into the groove of the second from right top peg, where you just ended, and hook the two bottom bands. Take extra care to push your hook down inside all the other bands looped onto that peg.

22 Loop the bands to the lower left. Be careful not to drop the bands off the hook because you are looping downward instead of the normal upward.

23 Push your hook down into the groove of the top middle peg, where you just ended, and hook the two bottom bands. Take extra care to push your hook down inside all the other bands looped onto that peg. Loop the bands to the upper left.

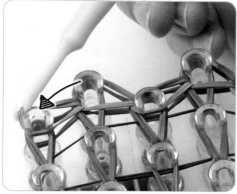

24 One more time, push your hook down into the groove of the second from left top peg, where you just ended, and hook the two bottom bands. Take extra care to push your hook down inside all the other bands looped onto that peg. Loop the bands to the lower left.

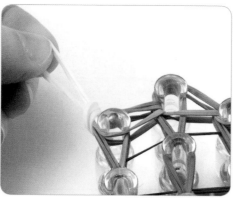

25 Make a slip knot through all the bands on the top left peg with three bands at once. This makes the robot's antenna.

26 Carefully pull the robot off the loom. Start by pulling the bands off pegs one at a time near the top, using your hook to help.

27 Leave the robot's mouth loose, as it is, if you want your robot to smile!

28 Or, for a serious robot, use the hook to pull the mouth through from the back to make it a taut, straight line across the front of the robot's face.

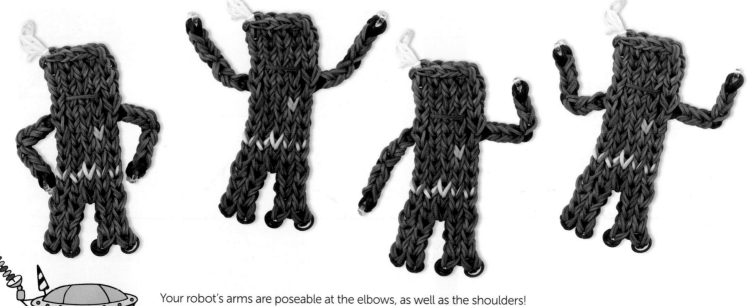

Your robot's arms are poseable at the elbows, as well as the shoulders! Make him wave, stick his arms straight out, or put his hands on his hips.

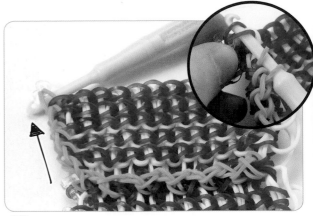

17 Make a connecting link through all the bands on the hook.

18 Remove the clip on the link you just connected to the stitch link to make sure that you connected them correctly. If it doesn't start to fall apart, you did it right. Leave the stitch link clipped for now.

19 One by one, stitch together the remaining five links on the top piece. Always push your hook through the next link up from the bottom, as shown. Always pull the new connecting link through all four loops on the hook. You'll make five more stitches this way. Remove the clips as you go. Then clip the final stitch at the top and take your hook out.

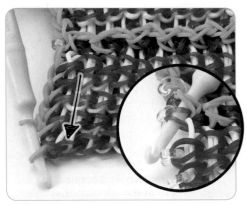

20 Repeat this stitching pattern for the bottom piece, starting in the middle with the stitch band you left clipped in step 14 and working your way down. When you reach the bottom, keep your hook through the last connecting link at the bottom.

21 Now it's time to cinch the top and bottom with connecting stitches. **Turn your piece 180 degrees** so that you are starting with your hook at the top right instead of the bottom left.

22 Without dropping the link on your hook (your hook should be facing up), turn your hook down and push it down through, not the link right next to it along the top, but the link **after that**—you are **skipping** a link. With the piece lying flat, you should be pushing your hook through the two strands of the link that are visible on top.

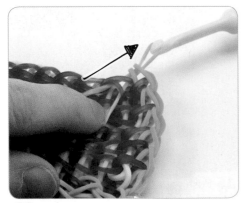

24 Continue stitching along the top by skipping every other link. Alternate pushing your hook up through the links and down through the links, as described in step 13. So, to make your second stitch along the top, you should push your hook up through the link, as shown.

23 Create a connecting link through all four loops on your hook. Skipping links like this is what will tighten the phone cover.

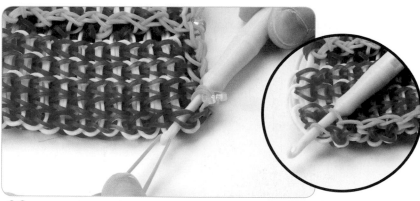

25 You'll make a total of six stitches along the top. **The last stitch will have to be right next to the link you just stitched,** because there is an even number of links to be stitched. Clip the last stitch and remove your hook.

26 Repeat this stitching process (steps 22–25) on the other end of the piece, starting from the bottom right where you clipped a stitch, and starting with your hook facing down through the clipped stitch and the second link (you skip the first). **Be sure to remember to alternate links.**

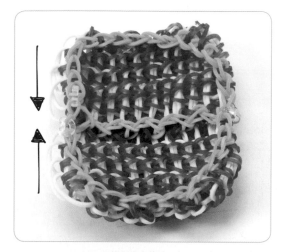

27 Now, from the top down and the bottom up, create connecting stitches between all 12 links on the remaining open side, as you did in steps 16–20 on the other side that was clipped. Make sure that you make these stitches through both of the loops of the links, as you did on the other side. You'll make 10 stitches this way (five from the top down and five from the bottom up).

28 Where the two final connecting stitches meet in the middle, push your hook through all **12** bands that the two clipped stitches connect together.

Note: For the fifth stitch on each half, push your hook through the very first stitch you made in step 10 before pushing your hook through the middle link. Then make a stitch through all six loops on the hook. This will make the case tighter.

29 Slip knot all these bands together and remove the clipped stitches.

30 Cut off the eight extra ring bands and remove any clips that are still on the cell phone cover.

31 Fit your new cell phone case onto your phone!

Rubber Band
Chain Madness

Floral Hippie Headband

Create a chain of 75 **double band** links, then slide two faux flowers onto the chain. Add or remove links as needed so the headband fits around your head comfortably, then connect the two ends with another double band link as shown in the photo below. Clip the last link closed.

152 pink bands, 1 clip, 2 faux flowers with loops/attachments on back

Fashionista Wristlet Strap

Create a chain of 40 **double band** links; add or remove links as needed so that the strap fits around your wrist comfortably. Connect the two ends with another double band link and a clip **around** the metal ring or zipper tab on your wallet/purse, as shown in the photo for the Floral Hippie Headband above. Then use a finishing band to slip knot the final link you just made and remove the clip.

82 black bands, 1 black finishing band, 1 clip, 1 purse with metal ring attachment or zipper tab

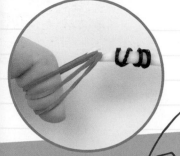

Trick Pencil

Start by looping a black band around your hook four times (see the photo above). Then continue by creating **triple band** links in the color order shown—two caramel links, 20 neon orange links, one gray link, and one pink link. Slip knot the final pink link securely closed.

1 black band, 6 caramel bands, 60 neon orange bands, 3 gray bands, 3 pink bands, 1 pink finishing band

Light Sword

Start by looping a shiny green band around your hook four times (see the photo for the Trick Pencil). Then continue by creating **triple band** links in the color order shown—12 shiny green links, three black links, one shiny silver link, and one more black link. Slip knot the final black link securely closed, and tie the shiny red band around the hilt of the light sword.

37 shiny green bands, 12 black bands, 3 shiny silver bands, 1 shiny red band, 1 black finishing band

Crazy Cool Cord Wrap

To make this cool wrapped cord cover, make two chains of about 60 bands each, then thread every link of each chain through one of the two split headphones cords, starting at the earbuds. Start a new chain of about 200 bands that connects the two chains where they meet at the split, then thread that chain through the main cord starting at the plug end.

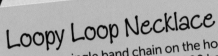

Loopy Loop Necklace

Make one single band chain on the hook that is anywhere from 300 to 1,000 bands long—as long as you want! Clip the ends together, and drape the chain artfully around your neck and shoulders.

Glam Beaded Curtain

Here is the biggest project you'll ever make using rubber bands! Create about 25 single band chains on the hook that are 300 bands long. (That's 7,500 bands!) As you go, loop each chain onto a 36" curtain rod, and then hang your curtain in a doorway!

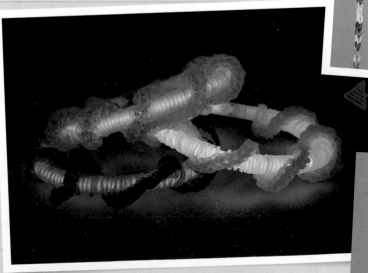

Wrapped Glow-in-the-Dark Bracelet

Make one single band chain on the hook that is about 100 bands long. Then thread a glowing bracelet through every link. When the bracelet fades, simply slide the chain off and put it on a fresh bracelet!

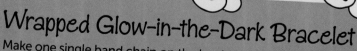